Made in the USA
Coppell, TX
07 July 2020

30381792R00066